MEET THE ROYALS

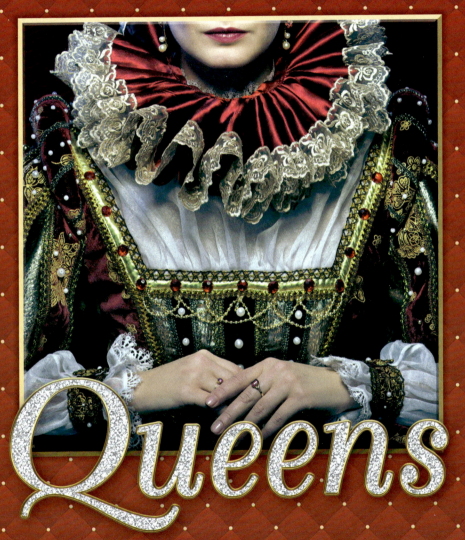

Queens

Enslow Publishing
101 W. 23rd Street
Suite 240
New York, NY 10011
USA
enslow.com

Sarita McDaniel

charity A group that helps those in need.

elected Chosen by a vote.

inherit To receive from someone when they die.

kingdom The area ruled by a monarch.

monarch A king or queen.

monarchy A country ruled by a king or queen.

reign To rule as king or queen.

royal Part of a king or queen's family.

title A word or words used with a person's name to show an honor or rank.

Contents

Words to Know 2

Head of the Royal Family 5

Who Runs the Country? 7

Becoming a Queen 9

Changing Laws 11

Marrying a King 13

Two Queens 15

Helping the Kingdom 17

Knighting 19

Sharing Power 21

Celebrating Citizens 23

Learn More 24

Index 24

Marie Antoinette (center) was a famous French queen who lived hundreds of years ago.

Head of the Royal Family

Kings and queens are the heads of **royal** families. Sometimes a country has a king or a queen. Sometimes it has both. In the past, many countries were run by kings and queens.

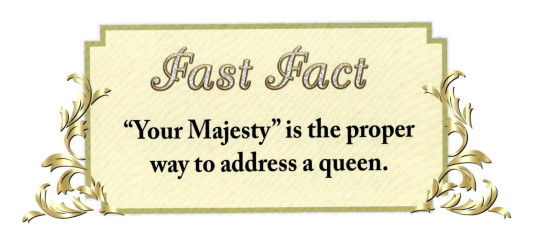

Fast Fact

"Your Majesty" is the proper way to address a queen.

The King of Norway sits with his son, who grew up to become king himself.

Who Runs the Country?

A country with a king or queen is a **monarchy**. A member of the royal family **inherits** the title of king or queen. The crown is passed from parent to child.

Fast Fact

Today, 44 countries have kings or queens.

Elizabeth II became queen in 1952 when her father died.

Becoming a Queen

The daughter of a king is called a princess. In some countries, a princess can become queen when she grows up. In other places, only men can rule.

Fast Fact

Queen Elizabeth II is the longest reigning British monarch.

Long ago, this castle in Sweden was built for a queen. The Swedish royal family still lives here.

Changing Laws

Some countries have changed their laws. They now allow queens to rule. But most monarchs are still male.

Fast Fact

Queen Elizabeth I did not allow anyone but royal family members to wear purple.

Queen Letizia of Spain has two daughters, Leonor (right) and Sofia. As the oldest child, Leonor will be the next queen.

Marrying a King

A woman who marries a king may become queen. Their children are princes and princesses. The queen teaches the prince and princesses how to be good leaders.

Fast Fact

Queen Letizia of Spain was a journalist before marrying King Felipe.

Crown Princess Victoria of Sweden is next in line to take the throne for her country.

Two Queens

Today, there are only two **reigning** queens. They are in Denmark and the United Kingdom. Princess Victoria of Sweden will become queen one day. She will be her country's fourth ruling queen.

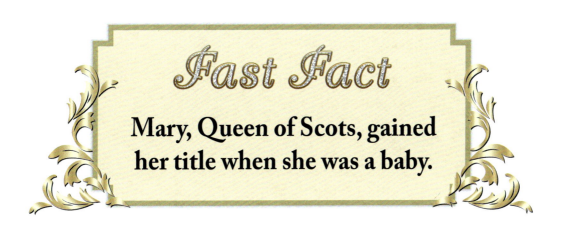

Fast Fact

Mary, Queen of Scots, gained her title when she was a baby.

Eleanor of Aquitaine brought new poetry and art to her country.

Helping the Kingdom

Queens have helped their **kingdoms** in many ways. Russia's Queen Catherine II made her country stronger and bigger. She also made sure more Russians could go to school.

Fast Fact

Queen Margrethe of Denmark illustrated the Danish copy of *The Lord of the Rings.*

The Queen of England gives the **title** of knight to British actor John Hurt.

Knighting

Knights used to be soldiers who would fight for the royal family. Today, the Queen of England can still give people the title of knight. It is a great honor.

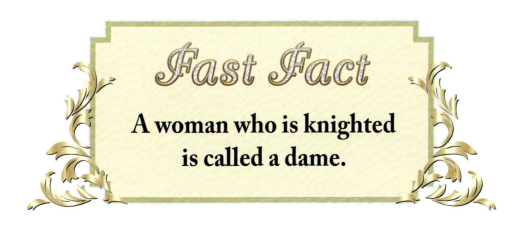

Fast Fact

A woman who is knighted is called a dame.

Queen Margrethe is Denmark's first female monarch since the 1400s.

Sharing Power

Long ago, queens made all of the decisions for their country. This has changed. People are **elected** to work for the country. The queen allows them to make most of the decisions.

Fast Fact

Queen Victoria started the trend of brides wearing white.

Queen Elizabeth II is the only female in the British royal family that served in the military.

Celebrating Citizens

A modern queen usually works with **charities**. She helps people in need. She also meets with the people of her country. She helps celebrate their good deeds.

Fast Fact

Before she was queen, Elizabeth II was a mechanic and truck driver for the British Army in World War II.

LEARN MORE

BOOKS

DK. *Castles*. New York, NY: DK, 2019.

Warren Drimmer, Stephanie. *The Book of Queens*. Washington, DC: National Geographic Children's Books, 2019.

Zeiger, Jennifer. *Queen Elizabeth II*. Chicago, IL: Children's Press, 2015

WEBSITES

The Home of the Royal Family
royal.uk
Find out more about the British royal family.

DK Find Out Kings and Queens
dkfindout.com/us/history/kings-and-quee
Learn more about monarchs throughout history.

INDEX

Denmark, 15, 17
king, 5, 7, 9
Marie Antoinette, 4
princess, 9, 13

Queen Elizabeth II, 8, 9, 18, 22, 23
Queen Letizia, 12, 13

Queen Margrethe, 17, 20
royal family, 7, 10, 11, 19, 22

Spain, 12, 13
Sweden, 10, 14, 15
United Kingdom,

Published in 2020 by Enslow Publishing, LLC
101 W. 23rd Street, Suite 240, New York, NY 10011
Copyright © 2020 by Enslow Publishing, LLC
All rights reserved.
No part of this book may be reproduced by any means without the written permission of the publisher.
Library of Congress Cataloging-in-Publication Data
Names: McDaniel, Sarita, author.
Title: Queens / Sarita McDaniel.
Description: New York : Enslow Publishing, 2020 | Series: Meet the royals | Includes bibliographical references and index. | Audience: Grades K–3.
Identifiers: LCCN 2019012397| ISBN 9781978511835 (library bound) | ISBN 9781978511811 (pbk.) | ISBN 9781978511828 (6 pack)
Subjects: LCSH: Queens—Juvenile literature.
Classification: LCC D107.3 .M39 2020 | DDC 321/.6—dc23
LC record available at https://lccn.loc.gov/2019012397
Printed in the United States of America

To Our Readers: We have done our best to make sure website addresses in this book were active and appropria when we went to press. However, the author and t publisher have no control over and assume no liability the material available on those websites or on any websi they may link to. Any comments or suggestions can be se by e-mail to customerservice@enslow.com.

Photo Credits: Cover, p. 1 Nejron Photo/Shutterstoc com; p. 4 Hulton Archive/Hulton Royals Collection/Ge Images; p. 6 W. and D. Downey/Hulton Royals Collectio Getty Images; pp. 8, 22 Tim Graham Photo Librar Getty Images; p. 10 Mikael Damkier/Shutterstock.co p. 12 Carlos R. Alvarez/WireImage/Getty Images; p. Pascal Le Segretain/Getty Images; p. 16 Heritage Imag Hulton Fine Art Collection/Getty Images; p. 18 © A Images; p. 20 Keystone/Hulton Royals Collection/Ge Images; cover, p. 1 (background), interior pages (borde Alona Syplyak/Shutterstock.com, cover and interior pag (decorative motifs) View Pixel/Shutterstock.com.

24